Y0-CHY-712

YAMAHA BAND STUDENT

A BAND METHOD FOR GROUP OR INDIVIDUAL INSTRUCTION

by

Sandy Feldstein
John O'Reilly

Welcome to Book 2 of the YAMAHA BAND STUDENT.

Your completion of Book 1 shows that you have worked hard and made fine progress towards becoming an accomplished musician.

The YAMAHA BAND STUDENT Book 2 will provide you with continued growth in developing a foundation for your future in music: as a composer, rock musician, teacher, conductor, symphony musician, or a listener enjoying the life-long benefits of music.

Your teacher's special skills, a fine instrument, your personal commitment and the YAMAHA BAND STUDENT is all it takes.

Continue your exploration into the world of music; it is YOUR world!

Sandy Feldstein

John O'Reilly

Instrumentation

Flute
Oboe
Bassoon
Bb Clarinet
Eb Alto Clarinet
Bb Bass Clarinet
Eb Alto Saxophone
Bb Tenor Saxophone
Eb Baritone Saxophone
Bb Trumpet/Cornet
Horn in F
Horn in Eb
Trombone
Baritone T.C.
Baritone B.C.
Tuba
Percussion—S.D., B.D., Access.
Keyboard Percussion
Combined Percussion
Piano Accompaniment
Piano Accompaniment Cassette
Conductor's Score

Alfred

YAMAHA®
is a registered trademark of
Yamaha Corporation of America

TRUMPET FINGERING CHART

index finger   middle finger   ring finger

O = valve up
● = valve down

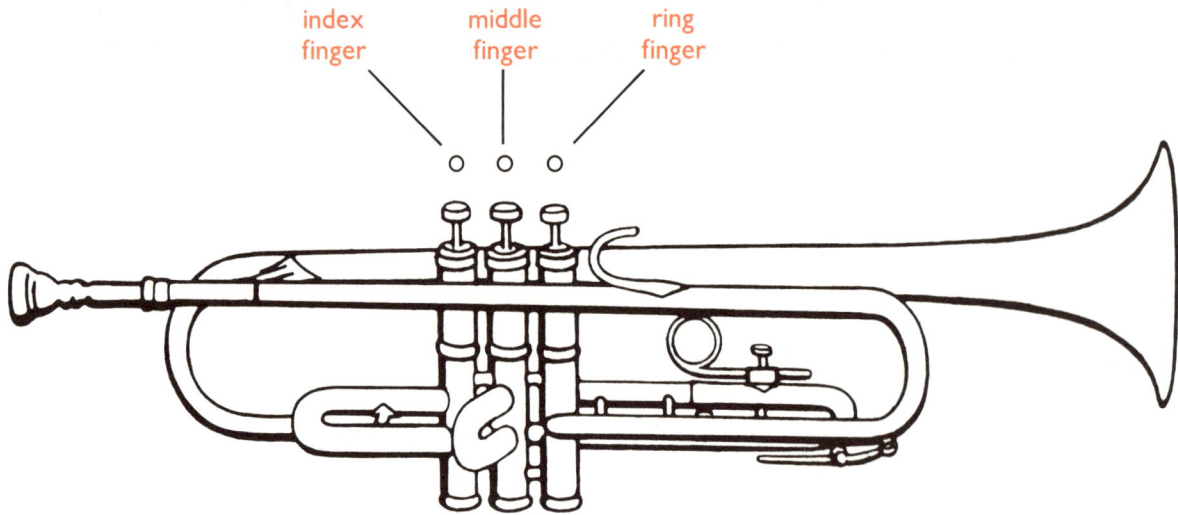

THE PARTS OF THE TRUMPET

Labels: mouthpiece receiver, mouthpipe, second valve, first valve, third valve, finger hook, bell section, mouthpiece, tuning slide, first valve slide, valve casings, second valve slide, third valve slide, third valve slide waterkey, tuning slide waterkey

STUDENT'S PRACTICE CHART

Name _____ To become a good musician you must practice every day. Find a convenient place where you can keep your instrument, book, music stand and any other practice equipment. Try to practice at the same time every day.

Week	MON	TUES	WED	THURS	FRI	SAT	SUN	Approval	Week	MON	TUES	WED	THURS	FRI	SAT	SUN	Approval
1									19								
2									20								
3									21								
4									22								
5									23								
6									24								
7									25								
8									26								
9									27								
10									28								
11									29								
12									30								
13									31								
14									32								
15									33								
16									34								
17									35								
18									36								

4

G Major (F Major Concert)	C Major (Bb Major Concert)	F Major (Eb Major Concert)

G Major Scale and Chords
(F Major Concert)
divisi

1

Michael, Row the Boat Ashore
Moderato

2
f

C Major Scale and Chords
(Bb Major Concert)
divisi

3

Deck the Halls
Allegro

4
mf g f e d c d e c d e f d e d c b b c
e f g a b c b a g
f g f e d c d e c

p d e f d e f g d
a a a a g f e d c

F Major Scale and Chords
(Eb Major Concert)
divisi

5

Carnival of Venice
Vivo

6
mf
>
>

Key Signature Review
Fill in your key name, draw your clef, and complete the key signature.

Concert Key	My Key	Key Signature	Concert Key	My Key	Key Signature	Concert Key	My Key	Key Signature
F Major	_____		Bb Major	_____		Eb Major	_____	

SYNCOPATION

D.C. al Coda (Da Capo al Coda)

Go back to the beginning,
play to ⊕ then skip to the coda.

1

Liza Jane

2

Alleluia

MOZART

3

Syncopated Duo

Duet

4

5

D.C. al Coda

⊕ *Coda*

D.C. al Coda

⊕ *Coda*

6

High Flyer March

The Streets of Laredo

Pomp and Circumstance
Duet
ELGAR

Just for Trumpets

CUT TIME

¢ = 2/2 = 2 beats to a measure half note gets 1 beat

1

Bb Major Scale and Chords
(Ab Major Concert)

divisi

2

Manhattan Beach

SOUSA

Allegro

3

mf c fed-dc fga-af edc-c e gab₂-b₂g

Give My Regards to Broadway

COHAN

Allegro

4

f c d e f g f

D.C. al Coda

Coda

Add the Bar Lines—Then Clap the Rhythm

5

8

DYNAMIC *ff* *fortissimo* very loud	**D.S. al Coda** (Dal Segno al Coda) Go back to the sign 𝄋, play to ⊕ then skip to the coda.	**TENUTO** Play the note for its full value.

Bb Major Scale Study
(Ab Major Concert)

1

Yankee Doodle Dandy

COHAN

2 Allegro *divisi* — 𝄋 — *ff* — *mf*

D.C. al Coda

⊕ *Coda* — *ff*

Dot-Dash Blues
Duet

3 Moderate Rock — *mf*

4 *mf*

ff

ff

FULL BAND ARRANGEMENT

A Joyful Chorale

J. S. BACH
Arranged by
SANDY FELDSTEIN and JOHN O'REILLY

Maple Leaf March

SANDY FELDSTEIN
and JOHN O'REILLY

RITARDANDO
rit. or *ritard.*
slow down

A TEMPO
return to tempo
(used after *rit.*)

1

Trumpet Voluntary

CLARKE

2 Maestoso

Fine *a tempo*

rit.

D.C. al Fine

Angels We Have Heard on High
Duet

3 Allegro

4

1.   2.

1.   2.

Just for Trumpets

SIXTEENTH NOTES

TEMPO

Allegretto
a little slower
than Allegro

1

The Thunderer

SOUSA

2 Allegro

Morning Has Broken

3 Andante

Listen to the Mockingbird

4 Allegretto

Add the Missing Notes—Then Clap the Rhythm

5

C#   **C#**   **D Major**
(C Major Concert)

1

The Minstrel Boy

Andante

2

The High School Cadets

Allegro   SOUSA

3

Nobody Knows the Trouble I've Seen

Largo

4

Dueling Sixteenths

Moderato   Duet

5

6

TEMPO

Vivace
very quick

1

D Major Scale and Chords
(C Major Concert)

2
divisi

American Patrol
MEACHAM

3

Merry Widow Waltz
LEHAR

4
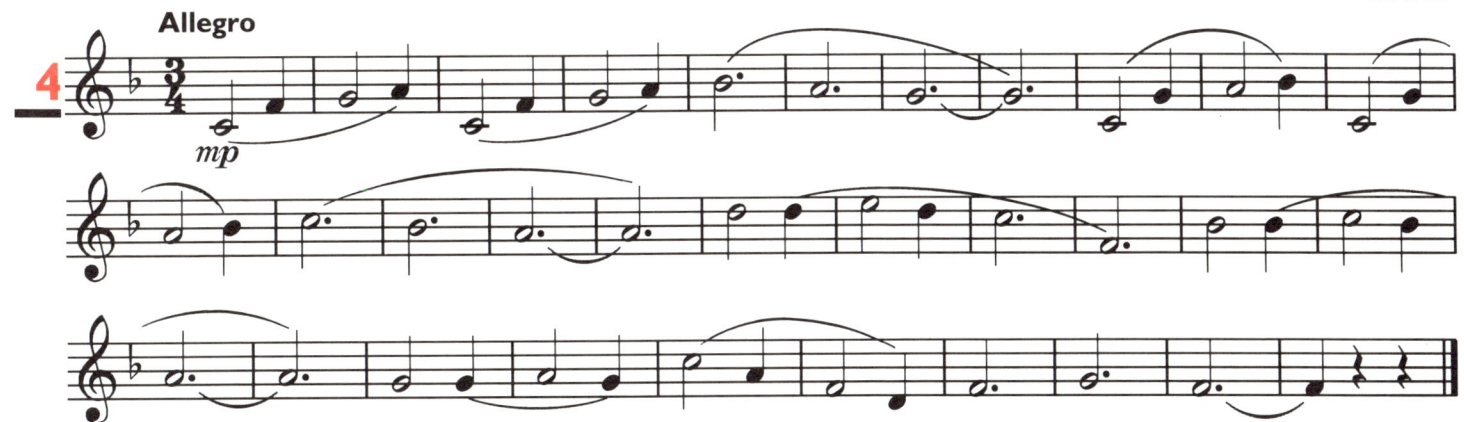

Theme from the William Tell Overture
ROSSINI

5

14

D Major Scale Study
(C Major Concert)

Little Brown Jug

Skip to My Lou

Just for Trumpets

Low C♯ and D are naturally sharp on the trumpet.
The third valve slide is extended to lower the pitch of these notes.

G Minor
(F Minor Concert)

1

G Minor Scale and Chords
(F Minor Concert)

divisi

2

Greensleeves

Andante

mp

3

Clapping Sixteenths
Hand Clap Duet

Allegretto

4

f

5

f

A Little Pop
Duet

Moderato

6

mf

7

mf

rit.

rit.

FULL BAND ARRANGEMENT

Hallelujah Chorus
from "Messiah"

G. F. HANDEL
Arranged by SANDY FELDSTEIN
and JOHN O'REILLY

ACCELERANDO

gradually
get faster

F Technic Study
(E♭ Concert)

Theme from March Slav

TCHAIKOVSKY

Maestoso

accelerando

This Old Man
Duet

Allegretto

Just for Trumpets

3/8 = 3 beats to a measure
eighth note gets 1 beat

D Minor
(C Minor Concert)

1

D Minor Scale and Chords
(C Minor Concert)

2

We Three Kings of Orient Are

Andante

3

mp

a g f d e f e d   a g f d e f e d

f f g g a a c b a g a g f e d d

The Irish Piper

Allegretto

4

f

Sea Chanty

Allegro

5

mf   *f*   *mf*

ff

Bb Technic Study

(Ab Concert)

Theme from Symphony #1

BRAHMS

Andante

Skipping Along

Moderato

Duet

Add the Bar Lines—Then Clap the Rhythm

ENHARMONIC NOTES

Two notes that sound the same but are written differently.

1

Our Director March

BIGELOW

2

Vivo

mf *f*

ff *mf*

ff

Clap and Play Duet

Andante

f

3 *f*

The Entertainer

JOPLIN

Allegretto

(E♭)   (E♭)

4 *mp* *mp*

D.C. al Coda

f

Coda

E Minor (D Minor Concert)

TEMPO Presto very fast

E Minor Scale and Chords
(D Minor Concert)

Three Blind Mice

Russian Sailor's Dance

Sweet Betsy from Pike

Just for Trumpets

1

Our Boys Will Shine Tonight

2 Allegretto

The Yellow Rose of Texas

3 Allegro

A Touch of Blue
Duet

4 Moderato

5

(C#)

D.C. al Fine

D.C. al Fine

Rhythm Addition

Answer each problem with only one note.

6

FULL BAND ARRANGEMENT

Stargazer Overture

SANDY FELDSTEIN
and JOHN O'REILLY

CHANGING TIME SIGNATURES

TEMPO
Lento
slow

Shenandoah

St. Anthony Chorale
Duet

HAYDN

Just for Trumpets

G#

1

D Technic Study
(C Concert)

2

3

Soldier's March

SCHUMANN

4

Allegretto

f *p* *f* *p*

f *p* *f*

The Stars and Stripes Forever

SOUSA

Vivo

5

f c c b a   a g23a a   a g23a a g23a c a c b♭ g g

(G#)

A

A Minor
(G Minor Concert)

TRIPLETS

A Minor Scale and Chords
(G Minor Concert)

1

2

Semper Fidelis

SOUSA

3 Allegro

Theme from Farandole

BIZET

4 Moderato

Triumphal March from Aida

Duet

VERDI

5 Maestoso

6

Key Signature Review

Fill in your key name, draw your clef, and complete the key signature.

Concert Key	My Key	Key Signature	Concert Key	My Key	Key Signature	Concert Key	My Key	Key Signature	Concert Key	My Key	Key Signature
F Minor			D Minor			E Minor			G Minor		

CHROMATIC SCALE

A chromatic scale uses all 12 musical notes.

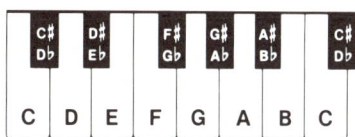

Chromatic Scale Study

1

March from the Nutcracker Ballet

TCHAIKOVSKY

Allegretto

2

Here We Come A Wassailing

Allegro

3

Movin' On Blues

Duet

Moderate Rock Feel

4

5

Bill Bailey

Presto

mf

Pop Goes the Weasel

Vivace

mp ff gg acafc ff gg af ff gg acaf fd1 gb af

mf ff dd egec ff df ec fb1 ab,cd1ef d1 gb1 af

He's Got the Whole World in His Hands

Rock Feel

mf da b d2 b g
d12

Hungarian Dance

BRAHMS

Allegretto

f

FULL BAND ARRANGEMENT

Blues Rock Finale

SANDY FELDSTEIN
and JOHN O'REILLY

TRUMPET SOLO

Two Baroque Dances

G.F. HANDEL

Gavotte

F Major Scale and Thirds
(E♭ Major Concert)

1

C Major Scale and Thirds
(B♭ Major Concert)

2

G Major Scale and Thirds
(F Major Concert)

3

B♭ Major Scale and Thirds
(A♭ Major Concert)

4

D Major Scale and Thirds
(C Major Concert)

5

G Minor Scale and Thirds
(F Minor Concert)

6

D Minor Scale and Thirds
(C Minor Concert)

7

E Minor Scale and Thirds
(D Minor Concert)

8

A Minor Scale and Thirds
(G Minor Concert)

9

YAMAHA BAND STUDENT

CERTIFICATE OF ACHIEVEMENT

has successfully completed Book Two of the
Yamaha Band Student and is promoted to Book Three.

_____
Band Director

_____
Date

Authors